Landscape from a Dream

Elisabeth Bletsoe

Landscape from a Dream

Shearsman Books
Exeter

Published in the United Kingdom in 2008 by
Shearsman Books Ltd
58 Velwell Road
Exeter EX4 4LD

www.shearsman.com

ISBN   978-1-905700-87-5

Acknowledgements
Some of these works, or earlier versions of them, have appeared in the
magazines *Angel Exhaust, Cambridge Conference of Contemporary Poetry 15
(Review 2005), Entropy, Odyssey, PQR* and *Terrible Work*, and on the websites
Tower of Silence (www.dhfurniss.eurobell.co.uk/esgardens.htm), *Great
Works* (www.greatworks.org.uk) and *Poetry International Web* (http://
uk.poetryinternationalweb.org).

A Spanish translation of 'Rainbarrows' by Ian Taylor appeared in the
Argentinian journal *Barataria*.

'Cross-in-Hand' was broadcast as part of the "Visionary Landscapes"
celebration on Resonance 104.4FM.

Contents

For my Mother and Father
and Ian

LANDSCAPE FROM A DREAM

After Paul Nash

*I dreamed about you, baby / it was just the other night
and most of you was naked / but some of you was light*
(Leonard Cohen)

I

intelligence   lies
at the edge of the body
    in the skin
along the littoral
feeling:
the weight of the cumulux
    hearing:
your tidal breath
filling my cavities
in liquid carbonic interchange

fissility of shale, its
    slaking,
plasticising when wet;
relict textures of petechial haemorrhage,

spermatozoa,
    saliva,
        oil
foliaceous, split-
layered like fingernails, revealing
the stem-ossicles of a crinoid
        ghosting

shattering
    with equinox

the black sand
how it eats up light,
abrades our flesh
        falls,
each separate grain
    in scratching atonals

marginalia:
    red & blond weeds
        sway at the shoreline
anastomose in a tholian
    web

a small boat
carrying the sound of your
        heart's engine

II

walled up inside
translute bricks of water
your hands make
    white shapes,
make a caress within
    an elliptical orbit of
        wave particles

making a slip,
    slipping in
grafting on a limb
to a limb, fused
   & drifting
       through the amnion
in marbrine light

above our bodies,
the underneath of the surface envelope
    is an ametrine laminate
      skin
now so rare & histamine
becomes palimpsest;
we write stories on each other

with our fingernails,
        red lines & white lines
dermographics
my name, Greek words,
      ciphers &c. on my thigh

dream of the stone
    lapis
the indissoluble self,
dream of the bull
    tauromachia
fear of incest with the father

initiations
   & a paring away:
we reach the chromosome body
in the nucleus of the organism

across the bay
activity without end
    but no volition
the machine pumps silently
pumping blood & oil

III

we expectorate the fluid
through which we have been breathing:
          the sea,
left to its volumetrics

we must suppress
the notions of childhood, that
     the hill
lives somewhere in memory:
when it appears before us
        climb it
but not to lose ourselves
     among the genealogies of dispossession

become avatars
put on animal masks
     falcon-headed
you are shadow-shooter, can
wound me & kill
        with a cast shadow
your manifold eyes, its
rutile threads vanish in
suddenly-expanding-black pupil:
       how it eats up light

in raptorous solar flight
through my nocturnal body,
    star-cell crammed;
proximity of blood and dung to
the interpenetrative organs,
        boli
carried on peristaltic waves
towards the horizon
    incandesce in the chromosphere

we must make it through the membrane
before the thing implodes, *AND*
    the fire that breaks from thee then &c.
red-red the sunrise
bleeds from my lips
        o my chevalier

IV

even the simplicity of light
    creates a choice
there being two types of loneliness, and
the second is that of
    lines & symbols
an absence of gulls' tongues
        de Chirico

spectral bays
plague-entrances the sea
        frays tenderly,
dark perplexities of seepage
from a loosely-knotted wound

and love a state of grace we are in
        its globes
tangle the uphill roots
in the vortex gardens of
the small coastal town, where
    we wait
among the architectures of barbarism
for the invasion of the horses

               *

the town is a lie, but
not a lie that can cause
        any damage

Purbeck coast from Swanage to Kimmeridge

Ooser

I

I was dead

but I survived myself:
risen altar of my own sacrifice

my hegemony precedes me as IHY son of HATHOR

I was the jacknife in the skybelly
"the Milky Way or conceptual stains"
an interpenetration around a constant (ga)lactic matrix

I slid forth from the effluvia between her knees' orogeny
I fisted out of the basalt egg; I oozed from her essence,
a chaotic from the sphere of entropy

I haemorrhaged in her blood

I am the master of redness
colour of nosebleed & cockscomb this side of abortion

I am the male of masculinity
Horn is packed laminate diamond tip drill-bit

I am the Bull of the Confusion
before the star-holes in the trepanned skulls of the gods
leaked the stroma of atomic glue
I am Himinhrjot, Heaven-Bellower

Blindly I dug out my own eyes
I morphed, waxed fat, I grubbed about, snuck
around, grew big
became a tall boner like my father when he tubered to his full

Horn devours inguinal soft spill cavity

swapped head for head, became Raven
became Occult, Soldier, Lion, Persian,
Sun-runner

sodomised the bride Khinkursag in Ur-metropolis

(Horn is the point at which my beastliness
hones its edge)

my neck got broke in the halls of the Mithraeum:
spinal ganglia germed the wheat that locked up solid got you
          to the land
my blood squinched from hypocythemic fox-grapes
burst scrotum spawned all manner of utilitarian creatures

splayed lascivious millennia frotting equinoctial fabrics
became part of the infratexture, bore
down on Betelgeuse / Bellatrix, dazzling acromion
K5 giant parallaxed in orbital fossa, while

Horn and its twin split the region
between event horizons and singularity

out from the tumulus
bucranium sprouts zygotic cones of focus
creates temenos/grave of light/absence/a dark & holy space
necrotaph to sawn grain, the screams of hacked
branches

severed wrist-stump sinks arterial roots down into the plough

a reversal of bones when
I clove deep shouldering the weather's slant

became rind thickened oak cortex
offered saprophytic feedings: leaves
eat air to exhale globes of jissom

(Horn is also the Open Throated)

I am URUZ
when I am whole I will
tear up the fallowlands

I am AUROX
when cut in pieces I will bind
the living

(reconstructed coffin-text)

II
strandloper

this is the story & the
bone it grew from

as septarian nodules accrete from
organic apices, flint forms about
a sponge gemmule;
    crack
open a chert knuckle   disclosing
crystalline structure of gastropod

          needle-fracture

on some rough quest to
animate the maps with my sperm,
        strandloper:
in the dead trench of morning
my bipolar shadow   howling
down its own demise in
forests of varicoloured consciousness

forests that start like
    the opening of language

from which a beast-form emerges;
decoding the spoor

> *snuff wind*
> *snotplug trickles into throat*

through cycads & conifers drowned in
cupressed silica preglass state
bunched as though blasted by a bitching westerly
   interleaved
with calcareous tufa, grasping into
soft aish where
fossil microsyllables spawn new cultures from
      milk & blood
over massed limestones
jointed   dissecting   breaking vertically
        away
oolithic structuring like
petrified fish-roe

growing a thin epiderm,
   upper grassy bevel
reticulum of *thymus*, trefoil & wild carrot
a treeless rind

sin-freighted, another   *soulbody soulbody soulbody*
erstwhile god in exile   *soul   all in tatters*
wuduwasa the satyr   *the holey man*

threw up the bank of Chesil
   overnight
much to the chagrin of the islanders
a high-minded race of Phoenicians

albedo rising from
wet   stone   glaze
a sound like the grinding of bones between
long canine jaws

a stone acreage
a people named for stone

(Stone, Pierce, Pierson)

those that lie in St. George's graveyard
choked on stone
dust   of centuries

in life I wroath in stone
now life is gone I shall be
raised by stone & by such a stone
as giveth living breath

the Stone Levy   the Bound Stone

scrobiculate, or
"marked with little pits"
a bone arena, cranium of Lazarus
light-shards flay the cornea, visual field scraped
down to the nitty-gritty   splintered
in my eye

unregarding of slip
& shift

on finding an adversary or obstacle,
demonise it & then,

powered by sacred names, beat it into the stone's
                    hard ministry

                TECTONIC
                FACTURA
                CONSTRUCTION

sublunary domination of a period
spent in Purgatory
        the "blood sacrifice"
sins of blood discharged in the body's exudate
washed away in the sweat *(sudor)*
 of enforced labour &
                learning

stone is polished by palm slime, the
                        sero-purulent blister

injury to the land analogued by
those convicted   harming their inner
flesh with concealed jags of zinc &
                        tin
men seeking cure by
being themselves carved out;
ragged by demons at great cost
                to the spirit

exolution in the apotheosis of the arch

the will to form of
the polyhedric crystal
        to become rock

"having the same properties in
   all directions"
its own elemental song
issuing forth between stone lips
resonant to the blow of the kivel
reverberant   through
haversian systems, periosteal cells
            into the scapular fossa

a chord that amplifies
with tidal pulsing, diurnal passage

coherent
frequencies   weather underfoot
      the electrostatic machine

octaves of infrasound
triggering complex repertoires in
my infected bullock's brain:
the clue that always leads to
      what has been forgotten

      BEATEN
      GROUND
      SCORED
      PIECES
      MISSING

labyrinthine stumblings
through the stone corymbs of
a baroque garden, silted
      chambers of ammonite
gyri branching to foliate petroglyphs,
holy transcripts, weapons of destruction

pterichthys, fish out of water
fallen fossil
             still falling

the light is also massive although
without weight

standing at the os
a perfect incised **A**   *is for Architect*
"increasingly vexed about
       various details"
his wineglass Wren-mark observed left
cut in stone within living memory

A for *Agrafia*, the places
                  unwritten

a navicular hollowing, stone   *oar-steed, surf-dragon*
ship-setting, a   *horse of the breakers*

scaphoid process; oak
sutured, cemented
       clench-headed, forced
              rib-cage
a framework of contingency
permitting the rain

water where none was
collecting   irrigating my desert fauces
the skin's necrotic sloughings
alembic potencies of tannic
       acids & calcium carb
ferment swarmed animalcules,

submerged reedlets   punctuate
insectivora at the surface tension

      stench of wet cow

"& we all went to heaven
        in a little row-boat", this is
the swan-lyric of Gokstad;
the prison-ship *Naglfar* built from
dead men's toenails; an invalid
hulk bearing the sequelae of rat-falls,
      obsolete fever curves

wreck of all wrecks, this is
the *Angel Guardian*, the *Hope*,
the *Columbine*, the *Arethusa*,
the *Charming Molly*,
    the *Forest* & the
        Avalanche
lost on the dark fields of the sea

     & the sea
gave up the dead that were in it
faces discoloured the nacreous
interior of a mussel, all
code, legacy & trace
   overscribbled by the waves'
      idiolalia
in constant erasure of the phenotype

    shattered skin;
      the crushed bivalve

those with hands
uncalloused   buried
to the north (my) side of the church,
the rest interred where they lay
            dismasted & disfigured

"that most dangerous of lee shores"
            notwithstanding
the sensuousness of its curve, the
symmetry of its crest, lack of lateral
edge   its rhythms of
            elutriation

from hence to seven miles distant
covered with the dead   bodies of men &
animals & parts hourly washed up
Nastrond, shore of corpses
            causeway of bones of the drowned, an
        inventory of loss

    "a peculiar kind of flesh-tinted jasper
            predominates"

                clumps of weed like
            tangled hair

I could not look back at the sea; I had
beaten the sea for myself but
only my self   everything else
            the sea took from me:

at the end of all rationalisation
the mass grave

                ★

pinched oval mouth volcanic
trickle rim crater bubble
extreme silky holes breaking through
well shiny pulling crackle glaze
lava lace pitted spiral outside stone

"persistent south westerly gales"
upholding the beach dynamic;
      flotsam   long enough in the Atlantic for the
                  efflorescence of goose-barnacles

          outposts
      on the borderlands of the real:

a trinity of lighthouses
foster a neurotic interest in
small migratory birds, the
snow-bunting &
        ortolan

nosing through disjecta, severalising
the uselessly wise from the
beautifully extinct

reconstructing clay &
wire hypotheses from a single
bone fragment, a
history from   scattered
        words:

          a beached wave
        a candle burning on the sea-bed
       an infarcted Luftwaffe bomb
         a plague-sore sealed in an envelope

making small breakfast from
salt-proteins of rock samphire, starched
root of *Arum neglectum*, we are

      malicious
because we are miserable   *tallet-shaker, gallicrow*

stranger to the breath of
my own relations, black

dog with eyes
as big as saucers snapping
rafty at my heels

I am swart, resented for
what I represent: your
hairy underparts   instinct for survival
become divorced from the squirming of
     cerebral coils, an
ignorance that ushers in whole spectra of
        dis-ease & pestilence

     monstrous omissions

a creature from the id,
as I approach
my bones turn to chalk, my blood dries to
inkstains on your fingers

            *

cursed is he
that removeth away the
mark of his neighbour's land

children bent & beaten
over the Bound Stone
"forcibly impressed"   with
          the weight of location

truly fixed
an ancient custom   time out of mind

III
schrecklichkeit

*"the **black** dog runs at night, the black **dog** runs at night*
*the black dog **runs** at night, the black dog runs at **night**"*

I was the end & the beginning; earthgrip, grimground, gravegrasp

I shaped weapons from hill to hill, letter to letter, point to point;
who but myself will resolve all questions?

I entered the foetal sleep of the warrior in the mound; dehiscent
skull cradled on my shoulder-bone

I was the gall in the ink of the *Chrestoleros*; that poor Bastard died
his head imploding with mad suns & marigolds

I chanced upon a girl alone; she furred hole vixen stank black
miracles

I was the ice cracked on November waters; that one was plounced
for a gig, a runagate, a speakarse & a baggage

I was the black car that sped from where Lawrence came to grief;
conspiracies flocked like crows in a welter of implication

I witnessed the brazen head when it began to speak: TIME IS, TIME WAS & TIME WILL

I swabbed the mouth of Mary Channing as she burned, her frightened nipples spat in the faces of the crowd: that made 'em jump back

I was the lead in the mercy-weights, the iron in the knife-blade & the scramasax

I took a boy unsuspecting in his cups & spilt the years of his disseminating gut

I was the pledge made to be broken; who but me rolled the Sherman tanks over Tyneham & Lulworth, turning you on turning you on to the military orchid

I thefted gold from a stronghold with no doors in marble halls as white as milk

I grew a hard-on at the hanging of Martha Brown; the rustling of her silks as she swang & twindled, swang & twindled in the breeze

I set the riddle: highty tighty paradighty, clothèd all in green

who said I had horns but was not a beast?

Interlude / The White Room
(hant: a ghost and its place)

St. Walburga's day came & went in thunder. Haruspication: a divination by hailstones. Not to venture across the threshold, invade the penetralia where paint scratchings become curls of eggshell patina infecting the nail's bloody sulcus. Melt of snowbroth and breakup of dendritic assemblies mosaicise hatshepsut skin. Mortmain. A certain antibiosis in arrangements of books & chairs set for the dumb speaker; a daily autism of the written page onto which the first horse-chestnut leaf is ritually pressed.

Absorbed in nephological study her reflected animus intercalates a finger inside her narcissistic wound. Deepening. Impossible to *undergo* without being physically changed. Oceans in freeze-frame aquarelle; the blunted hawfinch; the orangery transfixed under winterglass where vermin powderise root and quill.

A wilderness of doors.

★

Grief defined as the deferment of hatred/desire for ascendency, nurtured. The cadaverisation and artifice needed to maintain herself alive, but being beyond. Deepening, the pet cemetery; Goliath "beloved ferret". Points of centrifugal repulsion: the petty tyranny of some upper servant, faces made hideous by the marks of smallpox. A distant figure a tiny chessman moving against the sky.

Shrunk by the lens of memory, the rare overwintering of *Nymphalis antiopa*. Myth-imago; with each recital a layer debrided, releasing the one inside the one inside. The one inside. Until something black and solid crawls from the mouth.

Pruinate: hoarfrost, the appearance of being covered by. Roedeers' sharp-toed slots.

*

"The English squires are riding into the sea, most have already passed from sight...." Encrypted scattergrams of French boots & tulip bulbs along the shoreline from Worbarrow Tout. Attenuation of light passing through snow; absorption and diffusion towards an extinction. Fragile hollow cups forming, with lattice grains. *"... instead a dithering weakness that claws together some wool armour"*. A lower absorptivity in blue, deepening. Starfish, dogfish eggs, cryogenically preserved.

*

A process of sintering. Deep enough now to build a snow elephant.

Tyneham House

GAWAIN'S JOURNEY
"then thenkes Gawayn ful sone
of his anious vyage"

            "in low of frighting sky"
                        (goes
sodding up the) baulking scarp;
whale snout breaching shallowed seas of
                brashy soil
                        (jurassic coherence)
deepwater deposit of marl & limestone
ripple-stained by paleo-
                crystic tides

sway-back
                        clagged

trans / migratory beginnings, encroaching on
                the realms of silence, the
                        ghostland
effortful definitions
what it is
not   its non-existence

(the Opening of the Door)

"a hush, a sucking vacuum noise,
the sound of the cold, the landscape tensing"
sound of mortal
    disconnect

cervine figments
cervical spine flex(ual) split-
foot impressions in wet clay

to "travel light" in
foreknowledge of loss
to mark each path above &
    know
the underpath below
the route scratched in mind
like a line
digged in the dirt

"and uch lyne umbelappes and loukes in other"
chemical messenger dispatched
on the information highway

   logistics shook
  from folds of much-creased Ordnance map:

Beer Hackett . Knighton Farm . Limekiln Beacon . Honeycombe
Tout . Half-moon Clump . Jerusalem . Goat-
Hill Spring . Gospel Ash .

    synaptic junctures
   releasing their memory-quanta

hermetically sealed
below the clear transparency
            of consciousness
eyeholes torn
 in a mask of obligation
the journey narrowing vision
            until
                        only the road the
winding soil-tube of
Horsepool lane, Claypits
cyanosis of slathered leaves
"hazel & hawthorne harled all samen"

            mist-hakel

 a drippening muge of
 nucules, maple samaras; of
blackened stillborn eggs raining down
slicking clitoral tumescence of
prickwood arils,
            ranuncular coils &
                        scarlet entrails of Stinking Bob
"and all rypes and rotes that ros upon first":
phonerogamia   (melting)
                        the Perceivable Marriage

bone-mettled
the erotic impulse the
sprung energy
of a leap
                        arrested
transposed
along the tensile nerves
                        towards

barely perceptible
uplift of head

traversing her long back bone
where ribs of winter wheat
          articulate
toxic solanine shine of
dulcamara; flower-stalks
          ripening curve into
                    claws

          "slenderly entwined"

translating the protein chains
locked in the trees'
          incunabula;
crab apple's sour pentagram

the woodland draws from subconscious depths
                    therian forms, a
rider decked out in thorns,
equine muscle emergent from
Fuller's earth,
          dense holly infill

          (The Court Becomes Visible)

the blade mark a
love bite scabbed
          over
while the words dry with it;
the word is the harm
          & inside the harm

(He Strike the Blow)

the storyline bent out of true the
beast that waits in the clearing

    "the corsedest kyrk"
inside algal anatomies of beech, fleshed on
soil and light microbials   the
galvanic switch to breakout

        cleft-mast

engine onslaught of
      many-branched skull, twisted
black metal fingers grown webs of iron clutching
as visions sparking up
          escape the feral brain
    (error)
a careening off, cycle
    slipping a notch towards
        the fesse-point:

engorged transceiver of
  antler gristle
darker where more blood remains
      after brutal tribal combats:

the track of knowing smashed through
wild overgrowths of thought by
    long moons of repeating
means nothing
if it has no counter in this world
      wherein we walk and die

(home again home again
lickety-split)

Lillington Hill, 2/11/99
Day of the Dead

THE SEPARABLE SOUL

seepage

like the memory of water
an interstitial filtrate
        between stones, within speech

the weight of absence,
of meaning implicit in

                these empty spaces

reading you in
reading between the lines
absorbing small shocks of recognition that
        ripple back
from some projected future conflux;
sound-patterns skimming the surface like
        the dreams of fish

my interoceptors resonant with
vast electrical slippage
        down the sky,

avalanches of invisible lightning;
shifts in tectonic weather through which
I strive to detect your undersong
    in each volution,
        involucre;

to discover your cipher that
    I envisioned as
underwriting the disjuncted chancel, this
footprint of a drowned house,
    the seagrass meadows
"dotted with pulpy creatures
    reflecting
a silvery & spangled radiance
        upwards"

threads of occluded syllables
that bind me to the locale by
strange & injurious ties
    dissolve to
        incoherence
symbols like marks made by gulls in the sand

exploring the contextures of this
    erotomania
        (a nail in the vertex)
the exquisite salting of wounds

with each word I spoke
I was becoming less the person
    you imagined,
a second biography encrypted
beneath my skin:

as if I had left my heart behind in the wrong place

as if my lungs were too low and that something was growing out of my sides

as if I were in a cave of unknowing

as if a distance could be measured between hollow and holy

as if my chest were full of tears

as if my bubble were slowly bursting

as if there were a need for a lighthouse so we knew where we were

as if the third star were missing and I found it at the bottom of the bed

as if a light spiralled upward and opened my head; the dandruff of old snapshots showering down

as if on your own you really do hear voices in the tide

as if I were so isolated I could have walked into the lake

as if water swallows light

as if a central sadness coalesced in the sternum

as if the lights were switched off when I was halfway up the stairs

as if I were trapped between white sheets

as if there were something lodged in my throat like chalcedony as if the air had twelve edges

as if my head felt hot like a bird with high fever

as if a pain formed in my face in the shape of a bill

as if I were to start a soul-journey of a thousand and one days

as if while painting the ceiling white the marriage felt like a mourning

as if the moon had assumed the fullerine structure of consciousness

as if my cream silk clothes were covered in a huge clot of blood

as if a baby with bulging eyes were trying to suckle through its beak

as if I had broken an egg in my hand; a tiny white bird detached from
its yolk, breathing

as if this brackish lagoon were lipped by languages I was reluctant to
translate

as if in a dream subsisting on eel-grass among Siberian refugees

as if I were cutting apart two fish that were joined at the tails

as if a stigmatic inflorescence sprang from my right palm

as if there were a pulsating code at the base of the spine

as if white mucus dribbled from one nostril

as if a series of cuts had formed on the high arch of the palate *as if the* coles feminus *were coated in pearl*

as if I woke with the scrape of feathers between my legs

as if I were laying on folded wings

straying into the fault zone
as westerly cliffs of shear evolve
        points of collapse;
your leave-taking abandoned me
poised on the brink of a conversation
for which I now dis(re)member the
                language
scratches of light dissecting
the ridge of Corallian beds
        once formed in clear shallows

suffering attrition, a trituration
        becoming trite
detritus fetched up by the
overwash of storm-surge:
marine transgressions
inventing/reinventing my
                somatology
as the beach rolls slowly
        over itself
red & black chert, jasper, tourmalinised
                quartz

locus of transitions
a constant state of mutagenesis;
dialogue perpetually rehearsed
        but never spoken
tracing whole sentences

on the roof of my mouth with
                 my tongue
glossing over details that
you will neither read nor hear:

the inverse reflection of a tower cloud
            condensed
in a drop of rain on a reed-blade,
a floating quill plastered
to the smoothness of stone,
defence-posts of small bunting territories;

the capriciousness of the revealed world

my cell plasma preserving
            (it once was said)
a saline imprint of
                 that original sea

        all things tending towards solution

"tiny cuspate spits of gravel, limestone slab
        shells &
                 a little sand"

    the residew be sparkelid

Abbotsbury swannery; Chesil and The Fleet

BIRDS OF THE SHERBORNE MISSAL

I.

Unnamed, identified as Goldfinch *(Carduelis carduelis)*
for Suzanne

Days of brief transparency, viewed through a window of ice, lifted. Powdered across the lane. Having a porous cuttle texture as if drawn "using a thin & rather scratchy nib". A stricter regimen being currently observed, blood temporarily withdraws. Lenthay Copse smokily obscure. Brittle scrapiness of reeds, bones packed tight with air. Fish-spine delicate. A tenebrous rustle, like the breathing of books. Fields growing nothing but stones, bone white, buff white, ivory white, carved by the river Yeo, formerly the Gifle or forked one. Abounding in small flocks among the alders; a *c'irm* or charm indicating a tinnitus of small bells, blended, a continual weaving of waters. Angel speaks with multitudinous voice. "Thistle-tweaker", a conflation of thorns with the scarlet forehead becomes the iconography of crucifixion myth, ousting earlier fertile goddess affinities. Its nest a vaginal metaphor; a labyrinth of tender intricacies. *Lucina*, caged by the fingers of holy infants.

> sparkling up from
> the dried burdock heads, "a shrill
> piping of plenty"

II.
Roddok, Robin *(Erithacus rubecula)*

Becoming secretive & depressed in the later months, before the vigorous reassertion of autumn territory. Stakes & ties. Paths of observance newly laid through contusions of aster, sedum & verbena *bonariensis*, helmeted with bees; offertories yielding a roman tessera, three pebbles from Chesil Bank & a tennis ball. A smell of burning moxa. Sulphur being ground with mercury to form vermilion; glazed with madder, sealed. Red as a releaser (your fat cherry lips), the impossible fury of it all. Oscillograph of the throat, that bob bob bobbing thing. Boundaries constructed from scribbles of sound. Marginals encompass the crossing at North Road, where fifteen burials "very shallow & without coffins" marked the putative site of Swithun's chapel. Haunter of low places & diggings, befitting associations with early resurrection cults. A bird so hallowed such that, harming it, the offending hand would forever uncontrollably tremble. Bringer of fire from the chthonian levels, that our lives might blaze inches from shadow; burnt feathers colour of bright fame. Covering the bodies of the dead with leaves.

> tweezing grey hairs
> in the bathroom; outside a robin's
> winter song

III.
Unnamed, identified as Woodcock *(Scolopax rusticola)*

Being considered as late as the eighteenth century that they
spent their months of absence on the moon, an idea preferred
to the risible new migration theory. The declension from lunar
pastures, a glissade down streams of refrigerant light congealing
while filtered through earth's atmosphere. A millenial count
of sixteen on the Sherborne estate recorded as "noteworthy".
Frost-triggered, tumbled by Siberian winds; a fall, falling. Into
daylight hours of trance-like stillness. Lines of infection tracing
the foundations of the derelict war hospital. The isolation unit,
brambled. Aggregates of hyphae form underground cities of
mycelia; endless ramifications, the deliquescence of fruiting
bodies. Earth pigments, superfine ochres, sepia & sootblack
in a complex marbling. Almost present, not quite absent; *I am
not here, I am something else.* Limned in such manuscripts owing
to the succulence of their flesh; whole, roasted. Hepatic lobes
of beefsteak polypore exude a sanguineous juice; votive gifts
pressed into bark fissures: sheepwool, calcite chips, a palm cross,
attended by wasps. The pin-feather sought for its precision
fineness "to remove the mote from thy brother's eye"; mounted
in silver, to bring a woman to pleasure.

in my mind's
eye, brooding, a heap of dead
leaves on dead leaves

IV.
Stare, Starling *(Sturnus vulgaris)*

Ring-angels on the radar testament to starling diaspora. From the Greek, *psaros*, spotted or flecked. Hand against sky leaking through fingers; the point where everything breaks through. Refractive famishings. Flight as a single-celled animal, a granular flow into pseudopodia, pushing towards fission & fusion. The twisting of nuclei form trace-memories of divinatory meaning. Pound Road; domed canopy of the Monterey cypress, gravid with song, counterpointed by five flute-towers of Lombardy poplar in Blacksmith's Lane. Sugar of hedge-fruits turning to alcohol. Rumours of adolescent sciamachy; the stoning of hanging baskets, toppling of garden urns. Attempted gun-sales at Pack Monday fair; addicts buying lemons at local stores. The passage of saints-days in a watershine shatter of glass: Wulfsin & Aldhelm, Emerenciana & Juthware. Rough music, *charivari*. Ammoniac stench of the roost inviting various scatological nicknames. (Shitlegs). That petrol iridescence. A breast, "crowded with lustrous stars".

blackberry theft;
juveniles mimic Richard the
cabbie's ring-tones

V.
Waysteter, Pied Wagtail *(Motacilla alba)*

Ambiguities of black and white. Delighting in even a small &
temporary gathering of waters. In brief fugue through the
osseous bird-cage of the monks' lavatorium; an emersion of
helical patternings under the rain glaze on its blue liassic floor,
star-creatures lost in chalk seas in primordial times. Elemental
scratchings; refusal of the public-school boys to tread its deep
surface, architectural spaces infested with elegant & obsolete
ritual. Ancestral games. A sylph-like buoyancy against the
cohesive bulk of the abbey, internal voices transmitting its
prescriptive fictions. Darkening ghosts pasted to the weighted
song of the stone, damply. A conduit, to lead, but nowhere, of
the emotions; lengths being taken to avoid extremes, the careful
monitoring of lithium in the veins. Unwitting bride, squaring
up to the lens under Bow Arch, place of rebel execution. A
veil escaping in a stirring of winds; a bird in lovely & undulant
motion. Carrying within, always, the leaven of instant flight,
the announcing of wings.

> running running   shaking off
> three drops of devil's blood from the tail
>   tip

VI.
Mew, Gull (family *Laridae*)

Moving into the more solemn part of the Mass; gold foil running through the hedge, buffed by a wolf's tooth. Clifton Maubank, *Clistune*, concealed by dark flickerings of holly-oak; the storm horizon. Walled about with a batteled wall & "sette with all sorts". With naked foot stalking in my chamber. Legendary ash plantings, the once ever-open door. The writhe of negotiations & giftings. Alluvial soils, prone to flood: in fallow waves bathing, broading out their feathers among small flowering crucifers crushed by the hooves of cattle. Lustral gatherings; the flock a lucent stillness, heart's needle fixed to the south-east. *Varium et mutabile*, the cupreous light. A driveway, chagrined by leaves, pinnate & palmate. Breaking within, stone by stone, piece by piece, the structures of desire; the sun's low deception. Resteth here, that quick could never rest, *laros*, the ravening ones, implacable spirits of the drowned. An absent finial, a tree hairy with virus. The last worst enemy, to face impermanence; sunlight flash in a seagull's wingpit.

> "Sea-gulls, winter mews,
> haunt the fallow.
> Beetles flie."

VII.
Sparwe, Sparrow *(Passer domesticus)*
for Michell

Waiting for Sylvia, who never arrived. In back of *The Plume of Feathers*, a narrow sanctum in hibernal state, graced by the fluttering of small lives. Mimosa racemes. Roof-angles, at variance, drawn by the impetus of the abbey tower against ever finer & finer grindings of lapis & azurite. Into depthless sky. An insistent cheeping surpasses the bells' doxology; illicit couplings betrayed in a tremor of ivy. Naked stems of the winterstruck clematis proximate to the red bench, a simple narrative that becomes more complex; there is you, myself & many others like fingerprints among the lichen, staining. Faces that open & close. Things half-buried, annealed by frost. The inn a former mortuary, museum of autoptic secrets; no random event the disclosure of a statue of the risen Christ hidden within its walls. Sparrows gather, conductors of souls; only one human pair of eyes witnesses the child riding her trike across the flagstones. Back & forth, back & forth.

high gothic letters
blown by the wind; let sparrows
make a nest of them

VIII.
Heyrun, Heron *(Ardea cinerea)*

A page that encompasses the whole sky folds down to the shape of a heron, flying. Avian blood-cells a reliquary from cretaceous days; the serpentine throat, the gist of reptiles. Pterodactylar span devouring land gifted by Athelstan as barter for the soul's yearly mass; to Aenna's Pool, the Coombe of the Pigsty, Ecgulf's Tree, Aetta's Dean, "for all time". Pastures garlanded with wire & electricity. Barbed & tanged. Bird flesh that waxes & wanes in lunar synchrony with the lady's smock, vacillatory cress-hordes at the margins of the parish water-meadow. *Fons limpidus.* River-ephemera gather at Smear's Bridge; pollen spicules, florets of eltrot, a meniscoid bulging. The circumspect gaze; irides chrome-yellow, orbits naked, livid. From the banks of the Yeo, a stone frieze of three Magi, one bearing apparently a head, severed. A boy bringing to school a heron killed while attempting to swallow a live vole; the children of Bradford Abbas being "deeply interested in this riverside tragedy".

water glancing light;
    the long patience

IX.
Throstil cok, male Blackbird *(Turdus merula)*

Desultory & melodious with more intricate phraseology as the season advances; discarded notes upwardly forming invisible rooms of ancillary miracles in which to inhabit/yet to be built. Song-post on the Almshouse roof a nodal point above the facial ruin of a luetic angel. Imperatives from the Lamb & the Eagle. Reciting of our Lady Psalter five times daily in contemplation of death & judgement, a cloister of swept shadows. Trendle Street, Westbury; abandoned on unassuming corners, the simulacrum pertains. Teenagers dressed in rags of birds crowd the doorway of Docherty's Bar with aromas of batter & pea-wet. Distinctions elide between male & female, dark & light: [overheard] *"I'm in a state of flux right now"*. Apprehensions of subcutaneous violence like a distant bruise, a sky staining with orpiment. Budding yeasty moon under poriferous cloud. A saint opens a hand to find in his palm a small blue-green egg. Words thicken, unimportant & unanswered. Only being alive is left; the pulse, tic of raised tail-feathers on landing. Sung for its own sake.

midnight alarm-calls:
last bird of evening or
first of morning?

Maiden Castle

"you seem to swell so tall as a lion...
I fancy you would be a match for any man
when you are in one o' your takings"

let's toss as men do, ride
barebacked and astride,
the rinsing content of my soul
released to an eloquence of skin
rising in bubbles, an
artemisian rapture in
the miracle of self-
              examining:
I draw back my lips and
sunlight illumines the
      tulip interior

Thesmothete, I am
the law-giver, the beasts
are tarred with my
              glyph
where my boundaries intersect
gives meaning to your lives, pour
      ash, urine, blood

on the terminal stones; mark
the territory
             as dogs do

"& whenever I look up"
        your eye
at every crack, itching,
the prurient hole; the bride
stripped bare by her suitors
                draggling after me
the spoilt middle-class boys
who would emulate me, would
masturbate inside me,
        steal my words
but lose their coin of meaning;
                sensing
        your bone erection
        I turn and say, sit
                and swivel, honey

        (honey)

veiled, in tacta, I enter
        the nebulous swarm,
interpret the oracular
                voice of the hive
leave bee-cake and rags
for a town spread like a
dissected bird, canescent,

        gorge de pigeon

penetrate the septum, traverse
capillaries and venules:

Grey School Passage, Glyde Path,
    Icen Way,
             old wound-paths,
walkways of Jeffreys and Cheeke where
chestnut, lime, sycamore
    percolate
through a dense menstruum, deposit
          an auriferous marc

shards of Roman tile elude
 webs of superimposition;
    lacunae
cradle totems of the present moment:
woodlouse crumbles
        in loose mortar, goldenrod
sticks through
    curve and filament of ammonite
tracing the braille, book of the city
Colliton House wall, hard, stuff
that glitters, a compression
    of maricolous organisms;
         holiness and pollution

disease-repository of the museum:
"the brotherhood of iron, the metal of Los,
of cruelty, weapons, whips, the spindle of destruction,
the plough, chain, fetters, etc"

bull-stake. carfax.
the original church-triad,
    parish-markers,
half-buried dynamos pump their energies
(systole / diastole) along South walk
concentrate the brood-figures

of the Frink bronzes
"those of tender conscience
   martyred":
the deathform
reeks of male piss
         invisible ligatures

plague-scorch and fire-sepsis
form crusts of silence
among "pleasaunt town houses"
(a prayer-request at St. Peter's
       pray
for my husband who bullys me)
   and marriage, that's
a terrible wooden story
is *walled gravy*, stand
your ground and be cut to pieces:
the ritual slaughter of Mary Channing
abused arsenic-wife, cheered
by a "cast of thousands"
       Maumbury Ring
abcesses the consciousness
the air latent with accusations
is swallowed   is taint

       nobody can hurt a dead woman

the usury of sex   territorial
sniffings
the enclosure, terebration of
      the psychic envelope:
and whenever I look up
   your eye
inhales my presence, would

flense me with its shears
ram me with its telescopic lens
bore its gaze to my bones'
          diaphyses

not born to naifty, I walk the bund-path
round the city on the hill, the New Jerusalem:
queen of the cornmarket,
     the little gods of the fallows,
nightwalkers, swan-poachers and various
        shatter-headed persons

my skirt licks up scraps
     of libellous poems, my
footfalls like snowflakes
        in the ruminant dark
heart a mazed bird, my
palm holding a single grain
carp, pericarp, germ; the
        wonder of it
(my mind spreads away so)

"it is all that is made"

Bathsheba Everdene, 'Far from the Madding Crowd',
Dorchester

MELBURY BUBB

what belongs to me I keep:
my old love
where intimacy creeps
as if to a body buried
            in the woods

to become so lost so close to
where I started
encaged among the twigs &
    dormant buds
            like a great bird;
stridor of trees scouring themselves
    into wounds, the
tips of the branches breaking to
forked tongues of flame,
clatrian of sheet-metal foliage as a
cenozoic moon spirals toward
    fimbulwinter
into pitch scary black

    tallness
trying to pull down the sky
            with its iron claws

conjoined we were in this
a boundlessness of
    uncut quiet
contained in a single closed
                memory-loop,
the polarities of our exchanging thoughts
switching through umbilical corridors;

knowledge of *duramen*, heartwood
alburnum, sapwood;
abscission of leaf-fall
the tidal flush through xylem bundles,
slow accretions of lignin;
to plant in synodic rhythm,
                sidereal frequency
where grubbing roots knot spread matrices of
    blood,
            bone & gristle
ourselves & all we touched
grown from the one mesoderm,
    indivisible tissue;
an act to shake a single webstrand
            vibrates the whole:
    a lock of hair severed,
    a tree felled,
    a letter sent

        tiny instruments of causes deep in nature

this chalky knoll
"a multi-coloured fortified
    place"
flint-warted, gouged & rucked by
centuries of landslip
a hillful of trees thrust up;

writh & rowaty grass in
shades of buff, bistre,
    russet, rust & cinnamon
foxfire of deciduous larch &
out of the red the
    red dogwood a woodpigeon

        heavily

    & in all our outdoor days together the
    one thing he never spoke of to me
    was love
            nor I to him

where the antlers of an inverted stag
take root among
    ophidian coils
obscured by a sprung
            thicket of words
we carved a private alphabet,
residual meanings from
remoter signals of beech & sycamore
    "woaks & ellems";
now you have become your own myth, slipped
between cracks, into the void
            the ginnung-gap
myself left sole librarian of the codex of
    the scapegoated
    the bypassed
    the dispossessed

pheasant economies
preserving the land yet
    refusing access;

        social torpor
a parish adrift in its own dreaming
    swayed
by the stale exhalations of privilege, constructing
        an ossuary of bird-bones

ash-rind exposing its
    geodic core, broken
gate tears at my sleeve;
scrying among the flyspecks &
        amber rills
in the base of a cow trough for the
history of things to come

late oak eggar
knocks at my circle of light
set to die for what it craves,
that which is shielded from it,
denied it, would
            kill it
    if it ever did succeed

caught a falling star &
    cut my hands to pieces
a "heroic girl", an
unspilt vessel of silence
my years of backlogged speech
    grown calcareous like a
            stone baby

weighting you down
deep & safe in the
    grave of my thought
now you are mine & only mine

no other footstep
    could form its impress in
the leaf-encumbered chambers of
        my heart

in the chill beneath
the trees a mist becomes
    particulate, shines
my rough embarkened self
concealed as less than woman
        more than human:
earth gripped, this
grief, impacted, is what I have
    that is my own &
what belongs to me I keep

Marty South, 'The Woodlanders'
Bubb Down Hill

CROSS-IN-HAND

We find a short way by a long wandering
(Ascham, 1590)
for Margaret

no slack-twister I, see
my work-strong arms; gloves
   thick as a warrior's &
a rope of hair like a ship's cable

polishing grain against my side
my bones become milk:
see how the stalks
    imitate me
moving in the wind's electric spindle

working the ricks, binding
   sheaves to me, the
wrist's bare skin scarified by
stubble &
    the rain's arrows

To orient: to bring into clearly understood relations, to determine how one stands. Quincunxial signs I thread along by; A's magic well, church, folly, trendle, sky-notch. Beak through stone, the one who tracks me, and the other for whom I wait. High Stoy, Dogbury Hill wave a fringe of dark, concentrate the toxin rape-fields, xanthin & arsenic yellow. One field flares and then another, under the wheel of cloud. Drunk on rare pollens I would dance on this floor of lights, finger-hoops of earth spraying, apricot-coloured and friable. Serrated with pig-huts, dry as a kex. To study the architectonics of hog-weed. To unpack the poppy-bud of its outraged silk, corolla visibly hurt to the end of its days.

> I torce the necks of wounded gamebirds,
> shock of come-apart cervicals, reflex
>   wingjumps, (feeling)
> a pulse not my heart,
> the once-complete potential in
> soft declensions of egg-buds
>
> unspathing the spadix of
> wild arum   to bare
> male-&-female in one bulb:
> a scent of putrefaction &
> warm hairiness
> drawing flies across the meniscus
>
> the trees make eyes & leaf-
> edge water droplets have
> spirits in them of
> shone out light &
> I want to touch this to see
> what happiness is like
>
>   *"weighs on me more & more"*

what you say
a field-woman is a portion of the field
    "queer
      but tractable"
                as the hen-pheasant creeps
              stippled
a lost margin, imbibed
essence;   assimilated
& like the land tied and plashed you
appropriate me

        my body my sleep

no garden goddess nor Pomona;
my skin is beautiful
but nothing like the malic skin of an apple
and you wonder that I cry when you
        bite me?

The intricate hills a lament configuration. Lip of the downs I balance on, the calx escarpment; unlocking the puzzle below in reticulate fields, symbols to work by, a vibratory blue. Bata's Valley. Greensand & clay. The clunch tower breeding expanded atolls of white coral. Farms scratched up from chalk. A negative beauty in the straightness of a Roman road that rules itself out; puritanism scored on fields of wheat. Verges bleached to blinding. The scent of coumarin from trod grass (sweet vernal, false oat and fog), fills my head with a mess of leys and leptons, plasma currents and turf giants. Singing songs of a stone alone, never in one place twice, boundary of your craving. A marker, a "thing of ill-omen, Miss", covers the bones of one who sold his soul. Who walks there still. A galloping urge to rush into sky, to be taken up. Should I talk, at such times, of a sense of bruising, an isolation? It has to come to me, since, that I shall never be here. With you.

espaliered,
a fruit tree bearing pain's
white inflorescence, unfolding crimson
            stamen / stigmata
a collocation of thorns

quinque vulnera, the blood
stopt with webbing but
though I change / my womb changes
            lunarly
I am stained magdalen
with roots of madder &
                        green alkanet

dried on my thighs, rolling
pearls of slug-slime & cuckoo-spit
lactose of sow-thistle

to trace such "coarse patterns" on
            impressable flesh
my self bradded
                        & strent
energoumenos:
the one who is wrought upon

                        "Tess, darling Tessy"

grubbing swedes from the earth with my kisses
I split their hearts with my hacker;
in my sackcloth wropper
& curtained hood
a pasque flower, kneeling with
cries threaded through my teeth

enough grace & power in me to baptise my child
& then bury it
to turn my life about

*Evershot: "the place of wild boars"; Frome-source. Silvergleam bark
of ash lightning its shadows. St Osmund's gargoyles swallowed by
their own mouths; green men vomit leaves behind their hands. The
four Tetramorphs, visited by elderflower succubi, give way to creeping
necrosis. Swallows shuttle mandorlas of sound, dreamnets diverting
my prayers for a softening, a break in fixation. Waiting defines me.
Also a deliberate turning away before the goal is reached. Reinventing
myself. Flowering myself inside out. A hedge of floating calices; bride-
wort & wound-wort. Broccoli in my soup and from the open door of
The Acorn flow songs on the forbidden colours of love.*

"thought the soul was
an iridescent fish slipt
in & out the mouth"
blood-drips
a clepsydral measuring of
my life; a sound
            the size of a small blot
can shake a whole house

I will draw a veil over
my hat & black feathers, draw
it down to my feet
suspend myself
                reversed
for the journeying

under a killing moon
allotment fires break, fall
            gash themselves;
the fragmented bone-frame grown cool

among the ashes, the
likeness of an apple is
                then discovered
out of which a worm
becomes an eaglet:

at that time the flesh
        is born again jubilous
wholly renewed &
                        dissevered from sins

Teresa Durbeyfield, 'Tess of the D'Urbervilles',
walking from Cerne to Evershot

Rainbarrows

deep as the North star,
I can be neither familiar nor close

margravine of desert parishes;
places become crop-mark and
                                soil-shadow,
the lazarus-rattle of dried heather
as the wind slitters off from the Purbecks

adumbratio
I am veiled in a churchyard,
masqued at tide-times, a chimæra
vitrified at the window, eclipsed
by "disastrous twilight"

soul of all metals I am, but
"in a raw state" dreaming
the black stone of the self;
an idea seeking form as when,
above pondwater,
the ectoplasm of a projected leap
waits for a frog to flow into it

a few ounces of gorse flowers
and several parts each
        gravel, sand, clay
spread by glacial drift
        gravel-caps
plateaux separated by
slope-clays, loam-clenched fistfuls of
                shrub-tree
      cremation burials
an internal grit of crushed flint,
fragment of flanged bowl with
         painted wavilinear bands:
my stride devours the vell of the heath where
splinters of history continually discharge
at the surface of the present
    impatient   tracing the viper's keel,
slough of a lizard caught in rootwire
    a perfect replicant
Belovéd exorcist, what shall we call
this place of our rencounter?
                ("Bruaria?")
where we have never been is real

I have been pricked for a witch
    MERETRIX
                INSPIRATRIX
I can be your Turkish Knight
each corner of my mouth
as keenly cut as the point of a spear:
tiger-beetle, subtle in beauty
though I blaze under full illumination
brilliant in colours and
armed from head to heel

in gorget
        and cuirass:
                Venus as a boy

you cannot hurt me more
than I have hurt myself:
I have lanced my flesh with barbs of *Ilex*
burned my tongue with bearberry acid
tested flint on the edge of my palm
driven hawkfeather quills under my nails;
blooded, maculate in purples
I have prepared for my initiation
fought and fought to be
                a splendid woman

I will match you blow for blow
fain would I pierce, fain would I be pierced
infold and be infolded
eat and be eaten
flee and remain still
I loved a man once, and now
I love you
your thumb rowing strongly over my clitoris
                moving
from between my legs
to anoint my lips and cheeks
with my own chrism

swollen, we are twin horns
you standing at the mouth of a shining-walled labyrinth
where you can do what you want
do what you want
put your hands all over

                    and in me
o to be
o to be
to be your stunning
                    guide

you promised a thing not possible
a vessel of gold
twelve cities with a market in each of them
wrenskin shoes
a dress of wild silk
revolution and philosophy
you promised me and
you said a lie to me
now it's you are the lonely bird
throughout the moors and
that you may be without a mate
until you find me
                    again:

novembertime
when I will write my love for you in
fire across the sky;
chrysographer among stars like
flaming bees extinguished by the rain that
threads me back into the heath
sewn down to its magnetic core:
your port in my heavy storm
harbours the blackest thoughts, the
prow of my face cuts
        through its breath-cloud
I will name my ship
                    VICTRIX

neither life nor death dilute me:
out of suffering may come the cure

Eustacia Vye; 'The Return of the Native',
Egdon Heath, now Puddletown Forest

NOTES

Ooser

The Ooser rituals stemmed from ancient performances where hunters wore the skins and horned head of their prey in dances connected with their hopes for successful hunting and general fertility; the mask would also have represented a powerful nature god. With the advancement of Christianity this deity evolved into a devil and the Ooser, as it was known in Dorset, was relegated to the role of the Christmas Bull which roamed throughout the villages at the turn of the year demanding refreshment from anyone it met. It is likely there was some association between the Ooser and Jack-in-the-Green or the Green Man. The Ooser appeared on occasions of Skimity Riding in a gesture of derision towards adulterous couples and was also used to frighten miscreant children; the once triumphant horn of plenty, power and fertility becoming a symbol of scorn and horror. The word "Ooser" may be connected with "Wurse", another name for the Devil, also with "Guiser", an old word for a mummer. Originally, the mask would have been an actual bull's head, but later ones were made of wood with hair and horns attached, smoking lucifer matches inserted and jaws worked by string. The last one known disappeared from Melbury Osmond in the late 1800's; its eyes were said to convey an agonised spirit of hatred, terror and despair. The second section of the poem is set on Portland and informed by the Tout Quarry sculptures, the assemblages of Frances Hatch and the ceramics of Deirdre Burnett.

Gawain's Journey

Based on a piece of music of the same name by Harrison Birtwistle, with quotations from Alan Moore and the 14th century poem *Sir Gawain and the Green Knight*.

The Separable Soul

Since the swan moves in the three elements of earth, water and air, it has been traditionally associated with shape-shifting, especially in the form of a young woman. Tales of the animal-wife as swan-maiden occur universally, telling of a lover lost when she resumes her original form. Usually this is due to the lover breaking a taboo or committing a misdemeanour through a lack of communication, whereupon she diappears silently back into her supernatural life. I am indebted to Jeremy Sherr's Dynamis group for the homoeopathic provings of *Cygnus* which provided a starting-point for this text.

Birds of the Sherborne Missal

A missal contains the text and often the music needed to perform the Christian Mass throughout the year with variants for special points in the liturgy and for saints' feast-days. The Sherborne Missal was created in the early 15th century for the town's Benedictine Abbey. It is one of the finest examples of medieval book-painting and a major masterpiece of English art in the International Gothic style, its chief illuminator being the Dominican John Siferwas. It is "electrifyingly inventive" in its imagery and contains a remarkable marginal series of naturalistic birds, many of which are native to the area, and labelled with their Middle English or dialect names.

www.ingramcontent.com/pod-product-compliance
Lightning Source LLC
Chambersburg PA
CBHW031929080426
42734CB00007B/608